BOHEMIAN SOCIETY

BOHEMIAN SOCIETY

LYDIA LEAVITT

ISBN: 978-93-5420-694-8

Published: -

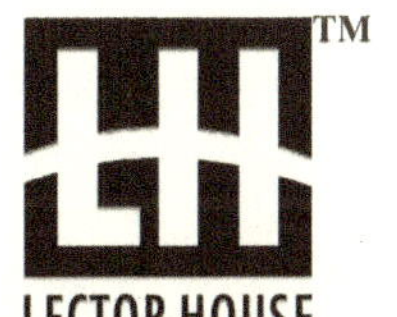

LECTOR HOUSE LLP
E-MAIL: lectorpublishing@gmail.com

BOHEMIAN SOCIETY

BY

LYDIA LEAVITT

BOHEMIAN SOCIETY.

"She was not fair,
Nor beautiful,—those words express her not,
But, O, her looks had something excellent
That wants a name."

In a country house near the city of B — — lived a lady of cultivated mind and manners, "a noble woman nobly planned." Well read and familiar with such writers as Tyndall, Huxley, Spencer and other scientists, and being rather cosmopolitan in tastes, liked to gather about her, people who had—as she termed it—*ideas*. At times there was a strange medley of artists, authors, religious enthusiasts, spiritualists, philanthropists and even philosophers. On the evening of which I write there was the usual peculiar gathering, and each one is expressing his or her views freely and unrestrainedly.

The visionary and dreamer said: "Let me describe a modern Utopia of which I have often dreamed and thought.

In a fertile valley, surrounded on all sides by high mountains, lived a community or body of people who had never been outside the valley. To them the mountains proved an impassible barrier and they had no wish or desire to penetrate beyond. For generations they had lived in this peaceful retreat happy and content. The ground yielded sufficient for their wants and needs. No one in this little world was richer than his neighbor and if one of the community fell ill each contributed something from their own supply for his or her support. They knew nothing about the value of money, for here it was useless. No one dreamed of possessing more than his neighbor, but each and all must share alike. Time dealt kindly with these simple people, for they dealt kindly with time, and life flowed on smoothly and pleasantly. Men and women of seventy years were hale and hearty, for it is not so much the *number* of years we live that leave their traces, as the events which transpire in those years; each event, each sorrow, each disappointment making an era and each one leaving a trace. For the inhabitants of the valley there were few disappointments and fewer sorrows. If the angel of death entered and took one of their number, each and all took the sorrow home for it was looked upon as a personal calamity when any one of the little community was taken from them.

The sun seemed to shine brighter, the water to be clearer and more limpid, the foliage more brilliant in this little world than elsewhere. Perhaps because the eyes of the people were undimmed by sorrow, perhaps because their souls were unclouded by sin, or perchance they were in complete harmony with nature and were able to see all her beauty, each charm enhanced by something within themselves.

Nowhere else did the earth yield such abundant harvest. The wheat bent its yellow head from over weight. The trees were laden with fruit and here again nature seemed to be in sympathy with her children. No sordid motives, no love of gain, no thought of barter and sale entered their minds while sowing their fields or reaping their grain, but every one labored that each and all might be benefitted. The men were strong and self-reliant, the women contented and happy, the children rosy and healthy.

Every Sabbath morning the old church bell rang a sweet summons to meet together to worship God. One church was sufficient for all. They knew nothing about heresies and schisms but assembled together to hear a simple story simply told. The venerable clergyman, with white hair and beard, in the dimly lighted church resembled the pictures of the martyrs, his face telling the story of a simple, true, pure life. His sermons were eloquent from their very simplicity; no need there of learned dissertations, for the people would not have comprehended had he been able to give them, and had they been able to understand, their pastor was unable to teach. It was a pleasant sight, the old men, young maidens, happy matrons and rosy children assembled together in their quaint old fashioned dress, simple in the extreme, listening to the teaching of their minister.

Their amusement and pleasures were simple with no unnatural craving after excitement. The ever changing sky and clouds; the mists on the mountain top; the purple hills and yellow waving grain; the running brook; all these were sources of pleasure and amusement. To a few, the world out side the valley, the numerous conjectures as to the people who inhabited it, gave food for thought.

At eventide the sun is setting, throwing a golden glow over the valley, from a cottage near is heard the cradle song of some happy mother lulling her child to sleep; in the distance can be heard the tinkling cow bell, and on the purple hill side the sheep have lain down to rest. The sun has gone down a little lower and the shadows of the mountains have lengthened until they stretch almost across the valley; the sounds of life have almost ceased; the child is asleep and the lullaby ended; the tinkling of the bells is scarcely heard; the birds have gone to their nests, and up from the valley has risen a white mist that has hidden and completely covered the last sign of life. Surely a beautiful covering for such a valley, a fitting mantle for so pure a people.

The morning broke dull and cloudy over the last happy day of the peaceful valley.

A stranger from the outer world, about which they had speculated so much, appeared in their midst. Seeking a number of young men he soon engaged them in earnest conversation, arousing their curiosity by telling them of the strange and wonderful things which transpired in the world beyond the mountains; telling them of the wonderful discoveries of science; the fame of many brilliant men and women, telling them of the advantages of communication with the outer world, of the uselessness and folly of spending their lives in so simple a manner, ridiculing their simplicity, telling them that the mere youths of his country could teach the venerable grandsires of the valley things of which they had never dreamed, telling of the advantages of extended thought and education. After many days spent in persuasion, he gained the consent of some to erect a large college which was immediately begun. Some of the older ones shook their heads and asked each other the question, "Were we not happy? What more can be required?" Thus the first seeds of discord were sown where all had been harmony. Laborers came from afar to aid in the erection of the college, and day by day the work progressed and children stood and gazed in open-eyed wonder at the place where they were to gain a world of information. The work was finished; teachers came from foreign lands, masters of languages, teachers of science, and metaphysicians to puzzle the heads of the old and weary the brain of the young. Teachers of music with massive organs for the music rooms of the college arrived, teachers of piano and harp, all of which were a revelation to these simple people, who could not conceive of any sweeter music than the song of the birds, their mothers evening hymn or the soft sweet notes of the happy wife as she crooned her babe to sleep. The children were sent to the college and and in a short time the strife began, each one trying to excel the other. No more time to study the effect of the misty mountain tops, no more time to listen to the songs of the birds, for here within these four walls were to be found and learned stranger things than they had ever thought of. After a few years the youths who went to the old church could scarcely be recognized. The same sweet welcome was given by the old church bell but how changed were the people who assembled together! Where all had been love and faith before, there was now doubt and discord. For had they not dabbled in science? Some of the more learned ones even whispered that the old clergyman should be replaced by a younger man, one more advanced in culture and training. True his head was bent and very grey, his hands shook and voice trembled and at times it was almost difficult to understand him, his prayer was so weak and broken. But at the bed-side of the sick he was always welcome, the infirmities of age were forgotten there. For over half a century he had held himself in readiness to attend the bedside of all who might call upon him to speak cheering, hopeful words to the dying. But now our little community has become educated and they are able to criticise. As we look around the church we are lost in wonder as to what has come to the people. The older ones are sadder and a spirit of unrest seems to have seized upon the middle aged, while the very children have lost something of their charm.

In a short time factories and manufactories are running; clouds of smoke ascend from the valley to the mountain top which had never been touched by anything less pure than the rain from the cloud or the mists from the valley below. Nature itself was making a silent protest against the invasion of her solitude. The trees which had borne abundant fruit before were barren now.

The older people shook their heads and attributed the cause to the doubts and unbelief which had arisen in their lovely valley. The more learned ones assigned the smoke from the factories to be the cause. Death was of more frequent occurrence to the inhabitants than formerly. This dread visitor came at rare intervals and to the very aged before the advent of education and commerce. But now the little children and youths were frequently stricken with strange diseases, which baffled all skill.

And after a time enterprise steps in and a railroad is built, and with it every vestige of the happy valley disappears. The old church is torn down, and a new one of grand proportions and elaborate workmanship is built on the old spot. The venerable head of the clergyman has lain low for many a year, and in his place stands an eloquent divine, with all the modern ideas, who, in trying to prove the doctrines of his church to be the true faith, leaves the doctrine of Christianity out— and that too has gone; buried beneath the ruins of the old church and in the grave of the old clergyman.

Now let a person pass through the valley and they will look in vain for a vestige of the once beautiful spot. There is a-hurrying to and fro. On the faces of the young can be seen lines of care and thought. The innocent faces and sweet manner of the young girls have given place to a look of consciousness. The pretty, quaint dresses have gone and fashion has sway. The quiet, dreamy look and manner of the young men has given place to a worldly air. The mists which arise from the valley are mixed with the foul smoke of the factories and engines, and where all was peace and quietness; chaos reigns supreme.

An enthusiast is saying:

Philanthropists in many ages and many lands have put forth great and noble efforts for the benefit of mankind and as we advance in knowledge and civilization the ways and means chosen have undergone many modifications. It has dawned upon philanthropists that they must have some knowledge of the religion of humanity before the change can be very marked, in the lives of those they would assist. The religion of humanity is the noblest, the grandest of all religions. It is the one which our Saviour taught while on earth; the one which he taught his disciples to follow; one which requires no trained intellect or cultivated mind, but simply an understanding of the human heart, the human mind, and human passions. In it there are no creeds to learn, no dogmas to understand, but the simple lesson of "Do unto others as you would they should do unto you," which is the foundation of genuine religion. Phariseeism is the curse of modern times, "Stand aside for I am holier than thou," is the spirit too often shown among—so called—Christians. The teaching of our Saviour; his life and good words mean little with many persons. The story of Mary Magdalen is simply a story, and conveys nothing to their minds. A supplication from such a one as she would meet with no return. The drawing of the skirts aside for fear of contamination, the cold looks and averted gaze, prove that at least, one noble lesson has been disregarded.

In the German town of Andernach there is a huge wooden image of the Saviour on the cross. And this is the legend which all the simple peasants believe.

"One stormy night a poor, sinful creature was wandering about the streets with her babe in her arms, and she was hungry and cold, homeless and friendless, and no one in Andernach would take her in. And when she came to the crucifix, she sat down on a stone at the foot of the cross and began to pray, and prayed till she fell asleep with her poor little babe on her bosom. But she did not sleep long, for a bright light shone full in her face, and when she opened her eyes she saw a pale man standing before her. He was almost naked, and there was blood upon his hands and body; and great tears stood in his beautiful eyes and his face was like the face of the Saviour on the cross. Not a word did he speak, but he looked at the woman compassionately, and gave her a loaf of bread, and took the babe in his arms and kissed it."

No need to talk of spiritual things to people who are suffering from hunger and cold. If the moral nature of the poor is to be reformed, their surroundings must be improved. "The mind becomes that which it contemplates." It would be impossible for any one surrounded by crime and poverty to understand or be made to comprehend the loving kindness of a God who placed them in such a condition and amidst such surroundings. No one, unless they were fanatics, would think of distributing religious tracts to the poor half starved ignorant portion of a large city. The *human* portion of their natures must be benefitted before any great results in moral improvements can be attained. Commence at the beginning. Teach them the laws of hygiene: teach them their duty, not from any reward which they may expect in the next world, but for the sake of right and the happiness it will afford them in this world.

I am often struck with the idea that the religion which is taught from our pulpits frequently helps to nourish all that is most selfish in our natures. We are taught that for every kind act we perform, we may expect a reward hereafter. In worldly matters we would have a poor opinion of a friend—or one calling herself such—who for every small act of kindness shown us, was constantly thinking of the benefit she was to derive from it. Why will the reasoning not apply to spiritual matters? Such teaching develops all that is lowest in human nature. And again we are told that by doing certain things which are sinful in the sight of God, we may expect punishment hereafter; consequently many people are deterred from wrong doing, simply from fear; not because of any inner consciousness of wrong doing, but for fear of the consequences of their sin. Would it not be well to teach and train the human mind to the belief that any act committed which is injurious to ourselves or our fellow creatures is wrong, because the act in itself is wrong and not because we are to be punished in the future.

Imagine a prisoner, a dangerous character, who conducts himself properly while under the eye of the keeper and in sight of the lash, compelled by fear to conform to rules, does the work appointed him, not from a consciousness of doing right, not because the doing right is a pleasure, but through fear of the consequences if he disobeys. He serves his time, is discharged, but what kind of a citizen does he become? If fear only restrains him from wrong-doing what object will he have in doing right? Leave out the doctrine of reward and punishment, teach and train the mind to something higher and holier than mere personal gratification. The religion of humanity is a grand, a noble belief. To remember that each and every one has some claim to consideration, that the way to restrain from wrong-doing is through the human heart. A warm hand clasp and a sympathetic tear will do more to strengthen ones belief in heaven than all the tracts which were ever written. Can we believe in the goodness and loving kindness of God, when we see nothing but coldness and selfishness in our fellow creatures. Ah believe me, the chords of the human heart are very tender and if touched by a sympathetic hand will produce sweet sounds but if touched by the unfriendly hand of coldness and indifference, the sounds will be harsh and discordant. There is no one so low, so ignorant, so fallen, but has claims upon our sympathies. The Turks collect every scrap of paper that comes in their way, because the name of God may be written upon it. Deal tenderly with every fellow creature, for all are made in the image of God. A few kind words have saved many lives from shipwreck. Phariseeism says to itself after hearing of the sin of some poor mortal "I am holier than that person. I have never sinned in that way," forgetful of the fact that they have never been tempted in the same way. The religion of humanity says "here is a poor mortal who has been sorely tried and tempted, we will show him his error and help him to do right." Phariseeism sends to the boy who has been arrested for stealing a loaf of bread, a tract with "Thou shall not steal" in large letters. The religion of humanity says, "the boy was hungry and we will feed him." Phariseeism says to the poor shivering outcast, "the Lord chastiseth those whom he loveth." The religion of humanity takes her in and clothes, feeds and warms her. To the poor woman who is struggling for daily bread, each day sadder than the last, Phariseeism says, "bear thy burdens meekly." The religion of humanity says, "we will do something to lighten her sorrow."

Phariseeism sees nothing to condemn in itself, forgetful that the sins they are committing may be greater in the sight of God than the sins which they are condemning in others.

I have often thought if a magician would wave his magic wand over a pool of water so that, not only the features but the mind, the motives, the passions were reflected, what consternation it would produce in the minds of the Pharisee.

O be charitable even as Christ was to the sins of humanity, be sympathetic even as He was to the sufferings of mankind; be kind even as He was to the poor; be merciful even as He was to erring women, speak comforting words even as He did to the weak hearted; speak cheerful words even as He did to the weary and sad.

> Who ne'er his bread in sorrow ate
> Who ne'er the mournful midnight hours
> Weeping upon his bed has sate
> He knows you not, ye Heavenly Powers.

Again the voice of the dreamer is heard. Let us, from a slight elevation, watch the busy life of a large city. At early morning can be heard the rattling of the carts and the merry whistle of the drivers—the red-faced market woman is arranging fruit temptingly in front of her stall; the shopman in a small street is lowering shutters from his windows; the little old wizened woman has seated herself on the curb stone with a small supply of apples and candy; the one armed beggar has taken his accustomed place; the shop girls are hurrying to their places behind the counters, the brawny workman with muscles of iron, strides along to his days labor, and all the work-a-day world is alert. A little later on the business portion of the city is abroad, the banker is being driven to his counting house, the wealthy shop keeper hurries to his place of business, and farther on the little flower girl with fresh violets, still wet with dew, can be seen with her basket, offering to the passers by the sweet contents. Now the great city is thoroughly awake. The miser and the beggar jostle each other on the crowded pavement, the little children are taken out for their morning airing by the white-capped nurse, a black robed nun glides along on some errand of mercy, with a face like a mediæval saint, jostling her as he passes can be seen the excited face of the gambler who has staked his all and lost, and again another flower-girl bearing her bright burden, now seen and again lost sight of, looks like a bright humming bird as she flits along, moving hither and thither in this strange medley of human beings. A group has gathered around some Italian street musicians; little ragged urchins are dancing in time to a merry waltz, and now the tune changes from gay to grave. Watch the expression of the dark-eyed harpist while he plays, surely his thoughts have flown to his sunny Italy, so sad, so dreamy is his look. Even this picturesque looking street musician may have a romance and may be dreaming at this moment of some sweet voiced Italian maiden.

Later in the day all the fashionable world is astir. Elegant carriages with gaily dressed occupants are dashing along. There is a carriage with the paint scarcely yet dry and seated within is a red-faced vulgar looking woman, the carriage, the horses, the woman, all painfully—*new*. At the same time hurrying along in shabby dress and mean attire is a fragile delicate woman whose garb shows evidences of much mending and patient darning, but the shabby dress cannot hide the fact that here is a *lady*, as with easy grace she moves down the street.

The afternoon is somewhat advanced and the occasional glimpses which we get of the flower girl show that her basket has been replenished but she does not move quite so quickly as in the morning. Her limbs are getting weary, and there is a pathetic little note in her voice now as she offers her flowers for sale.

But see! on the bridge is the figure of a woman. No need to hear her history, the face tells its own story of sin and misery. She is looking down at the river which flows sluggishly on; down perhaps at her own reflection in the water, down perhaps deeper still into her own soul. The face is hardened and set and there is scarcely a trace of womanly likeness left. A life of sin and shame has almost obliterated all that is good in her nature, almost I say, for no one, no matter how low or degraded, can be wholly bad. But here it is difficult to discern one soft look, as she leans wearily over the railing of the bridge—a silent, sad, sin-stained creature. Soon there is a sound of wheels and gay laughter and a carriage rolls by, and there can be no mistaking the nature and errand of the occupants. A young girl, with sweet, pure face, all in white, with white flowers in her hair and carrying a bouquet of white flowers in her hand, is being driven towards the church. Passing the solitary woman on the bridge she picks a beautiful flower from the bouquet she is carrying and tosses it at her feet, for she wishes to-day to make all whom she sees as happy as herself. A little of the hard look leaves the woman's face as she stoops to pick the flower. Mechanically she follows the carriage, with stealthy steps and bated breath she enters the church, choosing a dark corner where she will not be observed, she sits listening to the clergyman as he proceeds with the marriage rites and not until all is over and the lovely bride is passing down the aisle on the arm of her husband, does she dare to raise her eyes, and as she does so they meet the pure frank gaze of the lovely girl who smiles in her face as she recognizes the woman to whom she threw the flower.

The woman sits in her dark corner. Of what can she be thinking? Her head is bowed and on her face is a look of agony. What a hell has arisen in her breast! Her thoughts have wandered to her country home which she has not seen for years.—To the time when she was as pure as the young girl, who just pronounced her marriage vows; to the mother's blessing as she saw her young daughter depart for the great city; to the early days when she first arrived and worked honestly for her bread; to the pride she felt over the first money she sent home to her old mother. Her thoughts wandered back to the time when men and women turned to look at her fresh rosy face on the street, wondering at her beauty which partook so largely of the wild rose and mountain daisy. Could this be the same woman, with the hardened face and form covered with rags? It seemed so long ago. Then came the thoughts of striving with temptation, then the promises made and broken, of ruin and shame, then of the long illness, of dreadful poverty, and at last she sees herself as she is, a ruined, homeless, sin-stained creature. Oh the misery, the agony! What hell can be greater than this! While she is still sitting there the bell begins to toll, and soon there is a procession moving slowly up the aisle and four young boys are carrying a little coffin. It too is covered with white flowers, placed there by loving hands. In the coffin is a little waxen form almost covered with the same beautiful flowers.

The clergyman who had read the marriage ceremony, is now repeating the last sad rites for the dead. Again they take up their burden and move slowly down the aisle. As the coffin passes the woman, one of the white flowers drops almost at her feet. She stoops reverently and picks it up; almost hesitatingly as if afraid her touch will soil its purity, and placing it tenderly by the side of the bridal flower she walks slowly from the church. Watch her move along hurriedly, till she comes to a narrow alley and stops in front of a wretched tenement house. Entering quickly she passes up the rickety stairs and goes into a room where there is a little child upon a wretched bed. Sickness and poverty have almost finished their work. The child is sleeping and the woman steals softly to the bed side and places the white flowers on its breast Even as she does so the little creature smiles in its sleep. Perhaps the happy smiling face of the lovely bride has visited it in its slumber, or the spirit of the dead babe has come with the flowers, to take the hand of the sick child and lead it "across the river."

I hear the voice of the Pessimist.

Pessimism is increasing daily. Any person who takes time to think on the subject can not fail to see that human misery is increasing. With all the boasted advantages of civilization, it has failed to bring happiness into the lives of the people. The more enlightened people become, the more they will recognize the fact that knowledge does not bring happiness. Scientific discoveries do not tend to lighten the load of human misery. Since

> "Man's disobedience, and the fruit
> Of that forbidden tree whose mortal taste
> Brought death into the world—and all our woe."

sin has gone on increasing, consequently there has been more unhappiness. People are asking themselves daily, "is life worth living," and most persons answer in the negative. Are there any who grasp the prize for which they have struggled? If there are a few who succeed in reaching to the height to which they aspire, they find happiness is just as much beyond their reach as when they first started in their career. In the middle ages the magicians who created monsters were haunted by them forever after. We are all haunted by dreams and shadows. The dreams of happiness and the shadows of disappointments. Looking back upon our past and taking a retrospective glance at years gone by we find our lives have been made up not of *great* events—but of a succession of disappointments. Each one is haunted by a phantom or ideal which they are vainly striving to reach but seldom attain. The garden of hope seems to bear well; we put forth our hands to reach the fruit and we find we have only the ashes of Dead Hopes.

As Shelly says:

> "First our pleasures, die—and then
> Our hopes, and then our fears—and when
> These are dead, the debt is due
> Dust claims dust—and we die too."

It is bitter mockery to say that the man who struggles for daily bread is happy. He may do his work uncomplainingly, but he cannot be happy. He gets to be but little better that a machine and does his work mechanically, perhaps never looking into his own heart, to ask the question, "Is this a happy life?" Some writer has said that there are two classes of people, those who are driven to death and those who are bored to death. There can be no sympathy between the rich and poor. There is an impassible gulf that can never be crossed. The man who has never known the want of money cannot know the sorrows and struggles of the poor. Each must go his own way, the poor man to his pallet of straw; the rich man to his bed of down.

In the world of dreams all are equal. It is an unreal world, true, but to many it is the happiest. In it there are no distinctions. The woman who is old and wrinkled and gray, who has known nothing but hard work and sorrow in this world, in the land of dreams finds pleasure she has never known. In spirit, she is in pleasant places, carried back perhaps to scenes she loved in childhood, to the old home; sees pleasant faces of the almost forgotten dead, is carried above and beyond the world of reality into the dim shadowy land of dreams. Then comes the waking, and with the waking the regret of what "might have been."

In this land of dreams the rich may travel with the poor, may revisit the same old scenes, see the same faces of the dead, leave all that is "earth earthy," and the spirit or soul wander abroad, over land and seas and in dreams kneel again at a mother's knee repeating the prayer she taught and which has long since been forgotten, to awake with regret to the cares which riches bring.

There is one more journey which the rich and the poor take together and that is down and through the Valley of the Shadow of Death.

It is a curious study to watch the faces one meets in a large city or town. Every face has a history, every life a story, if we but take the trouble to read. The face is but an index of the heart, and even in the heart of the happiest the "muffled drums are beating."

As Longfellow so beautifully expresses it in "Hyperion" "and then mark! how amid the chorus of a hundred voices and a hundred instruments—of flutes and drums, and trumpets—this unreal shout and whirlwind of the vexed air, you can so clearly distinguish the melancholy vibration of a single string touched by the finger—a mournful sobbing sound. Ah this is indeed human life! where in the rushing noisy crowd, and sounds of gladness, and a thousand mingling emotions, distinctly audible to the ear of thought, are the pulsations of some melancholy string of the heart, touched by an invisible hand."

An Optimist, a pleasant, sweet faced woman, with a voice like the chime of silver bells, is saying:

"It is only to morbid and diseased minds that existence looks colorless. People who live too much within themselves, whose imagination becomes disordered see only the dark side of life. It was not intended that life should be all sunshine and no shadow."

> "For life is one, and in its warp and woof,
> There runs a thread of gold that glitters fair,
> And sometimes in the pattern shows most sweet
> Where there are sombre colors."

Dark clouds must appear in the life of each, and one of the great lessons of life is to learn to bear disappointments philosophically, not sit down with folded hands and watch the clouds approaching until our vision becomes obscured. There is sunshine in the lives of each and every one if they will but see it, and banish vain regrets and useless repinings. Inertia causes a vast deal of trouble.

> "Lose this day loitering, t'will be the same story
> To morrow, and the rest more dilatory
> The indecision brings its own delays.
> Are you in earnest? Seize this very minute!
> What you can do or think you can, begin it!
> Only engage, and then the mind grows heated.
> Begin it, and the work will be completed."

Fortunately the day of fine ladyism has passed and there are noble women who are not afraid nor ashamed to take upon themselves the duties and responsibilities of life, women who do their work well and faithfully, duties that perhaps in themselves are not noble, but by the manner in which they are done the work in itself is elevated. The common laborer who does his work well and to the best of his ability is more to be commended than the President who puts but half his energy in his duties.

What can be more pitiful than the apathy and utter uselessness of the would-be fine lady who is *ennuied* to the last degree; one perhaps with good ability who is conscious of the fact that she is capable of something better, would like to turn her attention to something useful, but is restrained from doing so by the fear of what "society" will say. Any society which is worth knowing will extend the right hand of fellowship to the self-reliant noble woman, much more readily than to the useless nonentity. Life to be pleasant must have an aim, an object, and every one has been given some talent to make use of and for such he or she must answer at "the last great day."

Life can not but be pleasant to those who make nature a study. There is a vast book open before us and every one who chooses can open a page. The study will never grow monotonous, for nature is constantly changing and with lavish hand showers upon her children from her great store house innumerable blessings, to those who "see books in running brooks, sermons in stones and good in everything."

From the fern by the way side to the study of psychology—the most fascinating of all studies—there is something in which all can interest themselves, but more especially for women, for to me this seems woman's kingdom. With much quicker perceptive faculties than men, they are better able to see the finer more delicate portion of nature's handiwork and mysteries. Unfortunately in small towns if a woman tries to investigate spiritualism, she is immediately called a spiritualist. If she takes an interest in mesmerism and psychology, she is called visionary. If she takes an interest in the religious discussion of the day, she is called an atheist. If she takes an interest in pathology she is called *strong minded*, and who does not abhor the so-called strong minded woman. A woman may be essentially womanly and take an interest in all these things. Brain was given to woman for reason and investigation, and "I rather choose to endure the wounds of those darts which envy casteth at novelty, than to go on safely and sleepily in the easy ways of ancient mistakings." Life cannot but be pleasant to those who are fond of books, "our silent companions." They speak a language all their own and we can find companionship for every mood, grave, gay, dreamy, discursive, philosophical and scientific.

If you are a busy worker in a large city and wish a breath of country air, a breeze from the meadow, a ramble along a country road, read Whittier's "Among the Hills."

> "Pleasant it was when woods were green
> And winds were soft and low,

> To lie amid some sylvan scene
> Where shadows dark—and sunlight sheen,
> Alternate come and go."

If you are weary with brain work and seek repose, read Longfellow.

> "And the cares that infest the day,
> Shall fold their tents like the Arabs,
> And as silently steal away."

If in an heroic mood read Milton.

> "For with thee
> Certain my resolution is to die,
> How can I live without thee? how forgo
> Thy sweet converse, and love so dearly joined."

If fortune has smiled upon you and flattery falls sweet on your ear, and you are in danger of forgetting the final end of all ambition read "Grays Elegy."

> "Can storied urn, or animated bust
> Back to its mansion call the fleeting breath?
> Can honor's voice provoke the silent dust
> Or flattery sooth the dull cold ear of death?"

If you wish to be transported to the mystic cloud-land of fancy, read Hawthorne.

"Sleeping or waking, we hear not the airy footsteps of the strange things that almost happen. He knew not that a phantom of wealth had thrown a golden hue upon its waters. Nor that one of death had threatened to crimson them with his blood, all in the brief hour since he lay down to sleep."

To a dreamy and poetic mind what can be more exquisite than these few lines: "The next morning Hieronymus put the scroll into his bosom, and went his way in search of the Fountain of Oblivion. A few days brought him to the skirts of the Black forest. He entered, not without a feeling of dread, that land of shadows, and passed onward under melancholy pines and cedars, whose branches grew abroad and mingled together, and, as they swayed up and down, filled the air with solemn twilight and a sound of sorrow. As he advanced into the forest the waving moss hung, like curtains, from the branches overhead, and more shut out the light of heaven; and he knew the Fountain of Oblivion was not far off. Even then the sound of falling waters was mingling with the roar of the pines above him; and ere long he came to a river, moving in solemn majesty through the forest, and falling with a dull, leaden sound into a motionless stagnant lake, above which the branches of the forest met and mingled, forming perpetual night. This was the Fountain of Oblivion. Upon its brink the Student paused, and gazed into the dark waters with a steadfast look. They were limpid waters dark with shadows only. And as he gazed, he beheld, far down in their silent depths, dim and ill-defined outlines, wavering to and fro, like the folds of a white garment in the twilight. Then more distinct and permanent shapes arose,—shapes familiar to his mind, yet forgotten and remembered again, as the fragments of a dream; till at length, far,

far below him he beheld the great City of the Past, with silent marble streets, and moss-grown walls, and spires uprising with a wave-like, flickering motion. And, amid the crowd that thronged those streets he beheld faces once familiar and dear to him; and heard sorrowful, sweet voices singing, O' forget us not! forget us not!' and then the distant, mournful sound of funeral bells, that were tolling below, in the City of the Past."

An artist is speaking:

A person may be a true artist, who has never made a stroke with a brush. Any one who can blend colors harmoniously or produce effective contrasts in dress, or even in so trivial a thing as fancy work, is an artist. Again, one may *paint* for years without the slightest knowledge of, or taste for true art. In painting a portrait, something more is required than the mere likeness, something besides pink and white prettiness. Perhaps in two or three centuries an artist is born, one who in painting a portrait produces almost a living, breathing creature; and is able by his magic touch, to paint in the thoughts which flit through the brain; the feelings which move the heart, and is able to read almost the very soul.

Many years ago a poor struggling painter in an Italian studio, conceived the idea of painting a picture of the Madonna. He shut his doors to visitors in order to give full play to his imagination. Days and nights were spent in dreaming and working, until he lost consciousness of the outer world and only lived for his work, for this picture, he was sure would make him famous. Days rolled into weeks and weeks into months, and still the realization of his dream seemed as far off as when he first began. The figure was standing with hands clasped and head bent in humble submission to the Divine will; the graceful, easy repose of the limbs, every curve and line was perfect. But the face! It seemed at times as if he had accomplished the great task, yet the expression always eluded his most earnest efforts, the heavenly expression of the Divine mother was wanting. At last, after many failures and vain efforts, it occurred to him to open his doors to visitors and perchance he could catch the longed-for expression from the faces of the women who might visit him. As soon as it was announced that the artist had opened his doors, people came from neighboring towns and cities, attracted as much by the desire to see the strange person whom they thought a monomaniac, as by the wish to see the picture. Women of rank and fashion arrived daily, and it was a curious study to watch the intent gaze which he fixed upon them, hoping, praying, in each one to find the desired expression. Occasionally he would request some beautiful woman to remain standing in a certain attitude, when he fancied he had caught the look for which he was striving, but it always proved unsatisfactory, for often the stately robes covered an aching heart which told its story very plainly on the canvass. Again a lovely girl would be asked to pose, but here alas was disappointment, for oftentimes the face expressed prettiness, but nothing more. Then again the canvass reflected the image of some worldly-wise woman with selfishness stamped upon it. Again the look of envy stared him in the face, or pride mocked at him while he struggled vainly on. As the last resort a young mother and her child were requested to favor him with a sitting. Here he thought

"I shall surely succeed." He worked steadily on and success seemed at last before him. The last stroke of the brush had been made and stepping back to view the work, his heart sank within him, for here he had succeeded in catching the look of lovely maternity, with the expression of the earthly mother imprinted thereon, but the combination of human love and Divine motherhood was wanting.

Just at nightfall, sick at heart, weary and discouraged, he wandered out into the streets, going on and on until he found himself in the portion of the city inhabited by the very poor; passing an old church, he was attracted toward it, scarcely knowing how or why. On entering the door, he saw a woman dressed in rags, kneeling before the altar. The man gazed in wonder and awe, for here amidst poverty and distress, he had found the expression vainly sought after, for weeks and months. In the face before him, there was no envy, hatred or selfishness, no vain glory or hypocracy, but the resigned look of one who suffered but bowed, meekly to the chastizement. At eventide, and alone, she had brought her sufferings to the foot of the Cross.

I hear the voice of the Cynic.

Friendship is a myth. In prosperity and sunshine you find yourself surrounded by flatterers and so called friends, but let the waves of adversity beat about and threaten to engulf you — then stretch forth your hands for the friends you have known and you will find yourself stranded and — alone. There may be a few timid, shrinking creatures who feel they would like to give the right hand of fellowship, but popular opinion and example prove too much for their weak natures and it is but charity to let them go.

"There are times when we are even inclined to smile at our own misery, but it is the smile which brings wrinkles instead of dimples."

The Philosopher is saying:

"Time in its resistless onward sweep" has taught us many things; has disabused our minds of many false ideas and erroneous views, has opened a new world to the thinking mind — a world of thought. When God created man he gave to him the divine instinct of reason, by which all persons, high and low, rich and poor, can solve for herself and himself the great problem of life. Very young children can only see objects that come within easy range of their vision; they are in the world of instinct, but after a time their vision becomes enlarged, they are able to see a greater distance, and in the larger space; more to arrest the eye — then comes consciousness. After consciousness — reason. The minds of many adults are still in their infancy, only seeing in a small circle the things by which they are surrounded and in close proximity. Others are in a state of consciousness and nothing more. They live, they breath, they have their being, but the great mysteries which surround them, the wonderful problems of life, are as nothing to them. Then again there is the mind that has reached the height of reason, and to that mind what a vast world has opened before it. The wonderful works of an all-wise Creator, the mysteries of nature that are so perplexing, are all open for the investigation of the reasoning thinking mind.

"The venomous insect beneath our feet, and the noblest and best of our domestic animals; the terrible forces of the earth, the tornado and volcano; the gently murmuring spring and the boisterous ocean; the forest monarch and the pale forget-me-not within its shade, are all witnesses of a creative power."

From the animalculæ up to Gods noblest work, man, there is the evidence of an all-ruling power and intelligence. Interwoven and interlined through all nature's great mysteries there is the mark of an invisible hand and all-seeing power, which rules and guides the universe.

> "That very law which moulds a tear
> And bids it trickle from its source,
> That law preserves the earth a sphere
> And guides the planets in their course."

It is by reason and investigation that we are permitted to partially understand the strange mysteries of a wonderful world. Each one must reason for himself or what better are they intellectually, than the child who only sees and cannot understand? Had it not been for investigation and reason, we would still have believed the earth to be flat, and in the rising and setting of the sun.

There is a law governing all things. There is a connecting link between earth, air and sea, between flowers, beasts and birds, between mankind and all animals, and inanimate things, a mysterious joining of mind to matter. It is an intangible something, perhaps an electrical current, but certain it is that the line is there and unbroken, and between every human creature whom God has made, there is the same unbroken chain, which can be followed up link by link, step by step, until we find ourselves on the boundaries of the next world and perhaps beyond; who can tell? The chain may be unbroken even then.

What matters it if I do not believe?—perhaps because I do no not understand your creeds, your dogmas. What matters it if I do not interpret the working of Gods ways in the same manner which you do?

There is the same principle guiding us all, and we bow the head reverently to the one God who "is the same yesterday, to day and forever."

Nations, like individuals, pass through the usual form of youth, manhood, old age, and decay. Religion, like nations and individuals, passes through the regular gradation, first of infancy, when religious ideas and thoughts are crude in the extreme; the age of Puritanism, when innocent women and children are burned at the stake for witchcraft, when with gloomy faces and in unsightly dress the poor fanatics sacrificed every pleasure on the altar of duty; the time when Sunday was a day of horror to children from its gloom, a day when every innocent amusement was forbidden. After religion's infancy comes youth. At that stage, the absurd dress and gloomy faces were not considered essential adjuncts to religion, but free discussion was not allowed upon religious subjects. Everything must be taken for granted, without any investigation on the part of the people. After youth comes manhood, the time when reason has full sway, when superstition and credulities form no part of religious teaching and thought. People are able to think, to reason for themselves. After the age of manhood, comes old age and that is the stage of agnosticism. Questions are being asked, and ideas propounded which must not be overlooked nor treated with contempt. All questions asked in a fair spirit, must be answered in a fair manner. It is not sufficient to say, "it is so", but good and tangible reasons must be given to prove the truth of an assertion. We are now in the stage of "old age." Agnosticism and Infidelity are wide spread. After old age comes decay and the decline of the absolutely orthodox. From time immemorial, every religion has passed through the same gradation, of infancy, youth, old age and decay finally comes *philosophy*.

A Swedenborgian is speaking:

Down by the sounding sea, in a lonely cottage, lives a woman, so wrinkled, old and bent that even death seems to have forgotten her existence. It would be difficult to imagine that once she was a beauty, but true it is that many years ago no fresher, fairer maiden could be found than this same strange old woman. Sixty years ago she had a sailor lover, who loved her truly and well. On his return after every cruise it was a sight to soften the heart of even the hardest, to witness the joyful meeting, the lovers kiss, in which there was no shame, the tears of joy in which there was no weakness; the heartfelt pleasure of two honest hearts. But the partings were soon to be over, for after the next voyage the young lovers were to be wedded. The simple wedding dress was made and all was ready. With gay snatches of song, and merry feet the young girl flitted about the house, impatiently waiting the day which was to bring her lover. There was only one more day of waiting and "to-morrow, to-morrow he comes," she sang. Early in the evening dark clouds formed in the sky, the wind began to moan, the waves beat high upon the shore, the murmuring winds changed to howling blasts, the waves rolled mountains high, the spirits of the sea and air seemed to have arisen in their fury, doors rattled, houses shook on their foundations—and to-morrow came, but no lover. The wedding clothes were laid away, and the day which was to have seen the young girl made a happy wife, found her a heart-broken stricken woman; and now she must take up her burden, and from month to month and year to year, carry this leaden weight called a heart.

The years rolled by taking with them her girlish beauty, and leaving in its place the wrinkles of time and sorrow. As time passed the idea took possession of her that her lover would still come back. True the vessel in which he sailed had been wrecked, but still there lingered the one faint hope, and every night she lit the lamp and placed it in the window as she had done in her youth, as the beacon light for the absent love. As time passed she followed her father to the grave and in a short time stood by the bed of her dying mother. And now she was alone in her loneliness and desolation. Every year when the day came which was to have been her wedding day, the white dress, which had grown yellow with age, was taken out, folded and flowers scattered over it as carefully as we would sprinkle flowers over a child's grave, for in the box in which the garment lay, were buried all her hopes. Does it not seem strange that one can live on year after year, with no hope, no joy; waken in the morning with the thought that "here is another day to be passed over," another night with the sad dreams and gloomy awaking.

At the approach of a storm, when the clouds began to gather, the solitary woman could be seen standing on the shore gazing long and earnestly over the dark waters. But at last it was with difficulty that she dragged herself to the beach and her hands trembled so that she could scarcely light the lamp for the window, but she said to herself "he will surely come," for if faith, hope and long suffering, if patient waiting, prayers and longing have power to affect disembodied spirits, my faith will surely be rewarded.

And now another year has passed and again the anniversary of the sad day has dawned. With trembling, withered hands, she once more unfolds the wedding dress. She must make one more visit to the shore, for she feels it will be for the last time, as with slow uncertain steps she drags herself along. And now as night approaches she is too ill to light the lamp.

Neighbors miss the accustomed light, find the lonely woman too ill to rise, and they know that in a few hours all will be over. They lit the lamp to humor the whim of a dying woman. The winds began to moan fitfully; the waves could be heard dashing on the shore, while the lightning flashed and illuminated the room in which the woman lay. There is something weird in the whole scene—the lighted lamp for the lover, dead over half a century, the dying woman, the moaning wind, and the sound of the waters. And now she is muttering in her dreams, and talking to her lover, she has forgotten all the years that have passed, and is bidding him a joyous welcome and while the storm is at its height, a smile of tenderness has passed over the face of the old creature, making her look almost young, when the door opens; a figure in a wet winding sheet, with hair in which was mingled sea weed, glides to the bed-side, a whispered utterance from the dying woman, "he has come," the figure moves again to the door. An invisible power has extinguished the light, and the flame of the lamp and the woman's soul, have gone out together, while from the bedside to the door there is the trail of wet garments.

Again I hear the voice of the Cynic.

This is an age of shoddyism, and it is difficult at times to distinguish the real from the sham. The woman who is covered with jewelry, looking like a travelling doorplate, is the kind from whom we expect the bow to vary, in coldness or cordiality, according to the clothes we wear, or the entertainments we are able to give. With such people money means everything, brains and breeding being secondary considerations. And it is very amusing on meeting Madam Shoddy to note the look with which she scans one from head to foot, balancing in her mind the cost of each article of apparel, her mind wholly given up to dollars and cents, and woe unto the person, who does not come up to the proper standard, of pounds, shillings and pence.

In talking with such a one you will find their conversation frequently interlarded with the use of the words *ladies* and *gentlemen*. But madam shoddy does really very little actual harm, all these things being a harmless sort of imbecility.

But at the hands of Madam Snob, one will not fare as well, for having nothing noble in her own nature she is constantly picking flaws in the character of others. Madam Snob will entertain you with a long account of her family connections. Poor soul she is constantly resurrecting the remains of dead and gone ancestors; her life is spent in the charnel house, being very careful however, to let the remains of a certain few rest in peace, while she rattles the dry bones of her favored ones in our face, until we are tempted to cry "peace." At last our curiosity is aroused, and we make inquiries as to these noble ancestors, and find the overwhelming fact— that they had been born! and that they had died! very noble of them to have been born, and very heroic, to have died. If the successors would follow their illustrious example in the last act, the world would still exist. But you say "this is harmless and only another form of idiocy." True if it stopped there, no harm would be done. But did any one ever know Madam Snob to stop there? After having visited her family vault, you are requested to enter the abode of your neighbor's dead, and then your turn will come next and you are asked by madam to unearth your dead. Now to people who know little and care less about their great, great, great grandfather, all this is very amusing. If the Bible be true, and who can doubt it? there was an ark built in which God's chosen were placed for safety. Now any one is safe in saying "my ancestry dates from the ark" but I think it would be rather difficult for a person to trace their ancestry from the time the chosen few stepped from the ark to dry land, down to the present time. But every one has some imag- ination, and in order to gratify Madam Snob's curiosity, just make use of it. Tell her some were hanged, some were drowned, some were in prison for debt, one fought in the War of the Roses, one was killed in a street brawl, another hanged for treason. Tell her—well tell her anything that will satisfy her curiosity, for there are times when an elastic conscience is excusable. There is another Madam Snob, who not knowing in the slightest degree what constitutes a lady, is ignorant of the fact that a lady is civil to everyone; this madam is uncivil to her servants, but does not hesitate to gossip with them, is careless, in speech and manner, in the presence of inferiors, in fact is guided wholly in matters of civility by the position in which the people are in, whom she is with; is constantly talking of *society*, and turning up her aristocratic nose at trades-people and in nine cases out of ten, her father was a cobbler, or kept a peanut stand, neither of which would do her any harm, if she only knew that "silence is golden." We say, *that* is the lowest form of *snob feminine* and rarely met with.

There is another form of snobbery which is not so easily recognized, and re- quires a good judge of human nature to detect. This Madam Snob is one who should be a lady, for by education and good breeding she is entitled to the name. Now, she really possess a good, kind heart, is kind to the poor, tries to do her duty, but away down, under several layers of good intentions, there is a little taint of snobbery, and she really has not the moral courage to rid herself of it. This Mrs. Snob may have a large circle of friends, but to each one she accords a different reception; to all she is kind, remember, but you can judge of her opinion of differ- ent ones, from the invitations which she issues. First in her estimation, come the fashionable people, those she asks to her dinner parties; then the people whose position in life is not very good, she asks to luncheon; then at last, come those whom she really does not know how to place, and they are the ones she asks to meet her alone.

Now this poor woman, for whom I have a degree of pity, not unmixed with contempt, is in a constant struggle with herself, in her desire to do what she thinks to be right, and at the same time, do everything that her neighbors do, for she is bound hand and foot and dare not make an independent move. But if Mrs. Fitznoodle were to do certain things, Mrs. Fitzsnob would follow her example, and the people who are asked to meet their hostess — alone, might find themselves seated around the mahogany with Mr. and Mrs. Fitznoodle and daughters and a select circle of little Noodles.

Again, Mrs. Fitznoodle, with several marriageable daughters, is constantly on the lookout for unwary young men, ignoring the fact of their want of brains, lack of breeding, and wholly regardless of the fact that they have no "family" connections, but she spreads her net and perhaps succeeds in catching this "eligible" young man. Mrs. Fitzsnob immediately sees something in that young man to admire, and seeks his acquaintance, and much to his surprise, and to the surprise of everyone else, he finds himself for the first time in what is termed *good society*. Now this Mrs. Fitzsnob is not a *rara avis*, but is frequently met with. Yet how many ladies do we see? We meet many calling themselves such, who do not hesitate to talk scandal, to injure their neighbors; to ridicule people, to accept of hospitality and comment ill-naturedly upon it, to talk slang. All these things and more, people do who call themselves, ladies. There are houses on which should be placed signs, as on pest houses, and whose occupants should be labelled "dangerous," for their tongues are more dangerous than the sting of the adder, and they are in so-called "society." Heaven save the mark!

Woman, the most perfect of all God's work, why do you not scourge society of scandal mongers, of snobs? Why do you not *dare* to do what you think and know to be right? Why will you allow yourselves to be ruled and guided by the opinion of others? A woman's instinct is her safest guide; if she follows it she will not err.

It is not women alone, who are tainted with snobbishness and shoddyism, but how frequently we see it in men, generally those who have very little brain and often in those whom the world calls self-made-men. Now there is nothing in the world so aggressive as the same self-made-man. The air with which he moves along, as though upon him depended the revolution of the world on its axis, and the safety and welfare of its inhabitants. He never allows himself, nor others, to forget the fact that he is self-made. The laborer, who, by dint of hard work and economy, has succeeded in making a little money; with what eagerness he tries to gain some petty office, and in a few years his daughters will tell us that they "belong to the old families." How much old families have got to answer for! It would sound refreshing in this age of snobbery, to see some one who did not consider themselves "as belonging to one of the old families." The male snob has developed within the past year, into the dude. By a process of evolution, which Darwin undoubtedly could have traced, we have him before us in all his beauty. To commence, first, he must have a little money, with that he buys a tight fitting suit of clothes, a diamond ring, a gold headed cane, a very small hat, carries his arms akimbo, and in all the perfection of loveliness, he stands out, a thing apart from the rest of humanity. Perhaps in two or three centuries, the process of evolution taking place all the time, something may be put into the small cranium, which will be called a "brain," but it must evolute rapidly or the sun will have cooled, and there will be another glacial period before that event takes place.

Then we have before us the man with three hundred dollars a year income, who apes the manner of the gentleman of leisure.

And now again we have what may be called an intellectual snob; the man who has a fair share of brain, but not sufficient to make a name for himself, not enough to make himself distinguished in any way. So where honest candor would expose him, he apes the manner of clever men, allowing himself to get decidedly "out at elbows," to wear clothes which decidedly require brushing, seats himself in a corner as though pondering some weighty matter, tries to look profound—when he probably looks simply, stupid. This is intellectual snobbishness. How many people we meet who cover their ignorance by a look of profundity.

When will people learn that snobbery is the evidence of a small mind, and that shoddyism is the proof of a vulgar one? How long before people will be convinced of the fact, that, education, talent, and good breeding, are the most essential requisites for success.

The psychologist says.

In dreams, and profound reveries we forget our surroundings, we travel over land and seas, through sunny lands, and many persons tell us that it is simply the mind which creates, the mind which travels. Not so; it is the soul which journeys forth and is actually in those places, having left the body while it wanders alone.

A person lying dangerously ill, suffering acute pain, is given a narcotic and after a time, sleep is produced. The pain-racked body lies there motionless as a lump of clay, pain is forgotten but the soul takes a journey, and for a time revels in joy, flits through a shady grove, or stops for a moment beside a running brook, scales lofty heights or lingers in a lovely valley; the effect of the narcotic wears off, pain returns and the pleasant vision is ended. Now the mind could not have created these pleasant scenes, for as everyone knows, there is complete sympathy between the body and mind, and a diseased, pain-tossed body, would produce a diseased mind. Between sleep and death there is a wonderful similarity. In sleep the soul wanders forth and returns to the body, in death it journeys over the broad sea of eternity into the great unknown. Have you ever stood at the bedside of a dying child and seen the look of joy that passes over its face? In many instances the child being too young to reason, too young to create for itself pleasant scenes. Then what could have produced the ecstatic joy? I stood by the bed of a dying child, a mere infant. The little sufferer had lain unconscious during the day, efforts were made to arouse it, the mother was bending over the bed anxious for one look of recognition, but the efforts were useless, the stupor continued until suddenly, to the surprise of the watchers, the little creature raised its hand, and pointed upward, with a smile of perfect joy, and at that moment the soul winged its flight.

Materialists will say the child had been told of the beauties of another world, and at the last moment memory and reason returned, and the beauties which had been depicted, were suddenly recalled to mind. But in this instance the child was too young to have been told pleasing stories; and the mind could not have created for itself a vision. Then what was it? At the moment of dissolution the soul had flitted through the gates of the eternal city.

A study in sombre tints:

In one of the large cities in the wretched portion where men, women and children hive together, there lived—or existed—a little boy, so small, so insignificant, that the people with whom he came in contact would scarcely have considered him worthy of mention. He was a wee specimen of humanity with flaxen hair and blue eyes, and people who stopped to notice him at all, saw something so strange, so pathetic in the childish look, that they involuntarily turned to look again. He spent the days selling matches; the nights he spent as he could, in empty boxes, on bundles of straw, in miserable alleys, anywhere, where night overtook him. There was no one to make enquiries, for he was alone, alone in the great city, alone in the world. One stormy night a woman found her way to one of the wretched tenement houses, bearing in her arms a tiny burden. One of the inhabitants, more kindly than the rest, took her in, gave her the only bed they had, a pallet of straw, on which she lay for a few days, making no complaint, giving little trouble. The women saw at a glance that she was a different order of being from themselves, that she belonged to another world than theirs. But by what chance had she wandered there? Questions were asked but no answers returned. She simply asked to be left alone. In a short time she died, leaving behind the little bundle of humanity, bequeathing to him nothing but her own sensitive nature, the same blue eyes and flaxen hair, and the name "Ned," nothing more. They buried her in the potter's field, and a life's tragedy was ended. Little Ned lived among them, getting more blows than kind words, nearly always hungry, but never complaining. If they gave him food he ate it; if he got none, he never murmured. The rough women, involuntarily, lowered their voices when little Ned was present, for there was something they could never comprehend about the strange child. They felt he was with them but not of them. He was unlike the children in the street, never seeking, but shunning their society. After a time he was old enough to go on the street and sell matches, and it was a relief to the women when he was gone, for then there was no restraint, and the little lonely waif was turned adrift. Little Ned seemed never quite alone, for he frequently talked alone, asked questions which seemed to have been answered—in fact lived in a world, peopled by his own childish fancy, and passed unharmed through danger and sin, where one, more conscious of evil, would have fallen. How unlike the world he was in, was the one he pictured to himself. At night he crawled into empty boxes, scarcely knowing what it was to go to sleep without feeling hungry, but the Goddess of dreams wove golden threads through the brain of little Ned, weaving her most brilliant colors, through the warp and woof of his childish dreams, as if in compensation for the sombre colors and gloom of his waking moments, and no child lying on his bed of down, placed there by the careful hands of nurse, and receiving the mother's good night kiss, ever had sweeter, purer dreams, than the friendless, homeless match-seller on his bed of straw. Mothers, do you ever think when you see your children safe in their warm beds, of the numberless little waifs in large cities, whose resting places are pallets of straw, whose good night kisses are the cold breath of poverty?

There was very little variety in the life of little Ned. Waking in the morning, he would start out with the matches, selling them if he could, if not, hunger, to which he was so accustomed, was his companion. So from day to day it was the same story, the only variation, the only change was in his dreams and visions; hunger could not deprive him of that solace, the cold could not freeze the warm fancies and imaginations. One morning in early spring little Ned awoke from his pleasant dreams and started on his route. Passing numberless people, some stopped to look at him carefully, for his face had such a strange look, his eyes had such a dreamy expression, and at times he smiled to himself as he moved along. But people did not stop long, for who in a large, busy city has time to enquire into the life and means of living of a little match seller. All day long, he trudged his weary way, and towards night-fall he found himself nearer the suburbs than he had ever been before. He passes a house which is brilliantly lighted, and strains of gay music reach his ear. Moving to the window, which was open, he gazes with open-eyed wonder at the scene within. It is evidently a children's party for little fairy forms are flitting about in a merry dance, and all is light, warmth and happiness, while outside with his face pressed close to the window stands little Ned. His flaxen hair is blown by the wind, his blue eyes open to their widest extent as he looks at the gay scene, of which he forms no part. Inside, all is happiness, outside is the gloom of night, and the desolate figure of little Ned. He turns away with a sigh, turns away from the happiness he has never known, into the darkness with which he is so familiar. He has grown very hungry, having eaten nothing since noon. Seeing a woman before a handsome carriage, he tells his story, but it falls on stony ground, the woman has nothing to give, and leaves him standing there, while she dries away. "O, the rarity of Christian charity!" Such are the women whose names very often head the list of subscriptions for Christian missions, but who turn a deaf ear to the sorrows of people at their own door; but if they give to the poor in secret no one will know it, while if they head a list with a large sum, they will be called good Christian women.

Little Ned starts again, trudging bravely on, foot-sore and hungry, and now he is in a strange part of the city, a place entirely new to him. A large building attracts his attention, and the sounds of voices reach his ear. Going to the door he sees a clergyman—a young man—talking earnestly to a group of rough looking men, evidently working men. The speaker does not stand aloof from them as though afraid to come in contact with them, but is talking freely, and has succeeded in getting their undivided attention, has won their hearts by his sympathy with them, has shown them that he is like themselves—subject to human errors and weakness, and these rough men are listening attentively, as they would never do to lengthy discourses about things of which they knew nothing. Here was a Christian—thank heaven there are such—who has not placed himself on a lofty pedestal, while the hearers feel that he is far from them both in heart and sympathy, but they feel that he is a man like themselves; he has touched the human part of their natures, and the rest will be easy. Little Ned listened, for the minister was speaking of things with which the listeners were familiar; of sin, of sorrow, of temptations, speaking cheerful words of comfort, leading them step by step to something higher and holier than they had ever dreamed of. At last, in language they could all understand, he told them of another life, another world where sin and sorrow could not enter. The child listened, and as he left the building hunger and fatigue were forgotten. Only half comprehending what the clergyman had said, only remembering in a confused way that he had spoken of a brighter world; one wholly unlike this one, one in which there would be no more hunger and cold, no more blows and harsh usage, the little fellow started in search, resolved to find it. Surely it could not be very difficult to find, and it must be some place outside this great city. Little Ned started on his search, going towards the open country, toward the place where the moon was rising, never doubting, never fearing, but that he would succeed. Day after day he wandered on, eating berries which he found by the wayside, and occasionally asking for something to eat. He slept in the open air, for he knew no fear; his brain still weaving the golden threads; still talking to invisible spirits; his face looking so spiritual that one was not surprised that strange tongues spoke a strange language to the lonely boy. He has wandered on until his feet are sore and a feeling of weariness steals over him; he looks around and finds that he is no nearer than when he started to the bright world which the clergyman had talked about. So he resolves to turn, to go back to the place where he had seen the minister, and ask him to show him the way. Back he turns on his long journey. Step by step, slowly and wearily he trudges along, his eyes have grown larger, his skin more transparent, and each day finds him a little weaker, but he feels that he must go on. Strange voices are speaking to him more frequently than ever, and his dreams are filled with visions of the new world of which he has heard, and now he has almost reached his journeys end, but it requires a great effort for him to move, he is so foot-sore and weary, but the voices are urging him on and at last the building is in sight. He drags himself wearily to the door. It is night and the door is open—the place is deserted, but he throws himself down on the floor with a sigh of contentment. The next morning they found him with his hands clasped and face upturned to the skies. The blue eyes were opened wide, the lips parted in a happy smile, and poor little lonely Ned had found the "bright world."

The Poet says:

So many abler tongues and pens than mine have chosen the St. Lawrence as a theme on which they have written love songs, romances and legends, that it would ill-become me to even attempt the subject. A writer, many years ago, while paddling up the river and among the Islands, expressed himself thus: "As the sun set below the islands the full moon rose in all her beauty. The light evening breeze had subsided into a calm; not a breath of air ruffled the glassy waters.

Impressed with the solemnity of the scene, I could not refrain from wishing that here, at least, Nature might be permitted to reign unmolested, but the solitary watch-fires of the recent settlers gave proof that though his tenure was yet but frail, man! rapacious and indefatigable man! was fast establishing usurpation." This was written many years ago. What would be the astonishment of the writer, if he could revisit the scene. Would he think it improvement or desecration? On the islands cottages are built, and well kept lawns, sloping down to the water, are brightened by the bright dresses of women and children, and in some places the modern game of lawn tennis is being played, and everything shows that Nature has not been allowed to reign unmolested. Steamboats are plying from place to place; pleasure seekers lift their voices to hear the sounds re-echoed from island to island, from shore to shore, until the faint reverberation is lost among the murmuring pines. Surely the crags and trees, the pines and poplars, are tempted to return the echo as a protest against this invasion. If the sensibilities were quickened to the sounds of nature, the words re-echoed would be "leave us alone in our solitude."

The St. Lawrence does not speak to our hearts of deep tragedies, but breathes into the soul a spirit of love.

"When Eve plucked death from the tree of life and brought tears of sorrow upon earth, Adam was driven out into the world to mourn with her, and taste from the bitter spring that we drink to-day."

"Then angels on their wings, bore the silent Eden to the eternal spheres on high, and placed it in the heavens—but in passing through space, they dropped along the way, to mark their course, some flowers from the garden divine. These flowers of changing hues, falling into the great river, became the Thousand Isles— the Paradise of the St. Lawrence."

It is a study to watch the different expressions and manners of the people whom we meet. There is the woman who, on meeting makes one feel that they have passed through some difficult surgical operation, her look is so hard and penetrating, like the surgeon's knife. Then another with an expression so benevolent, so charitable, that one is inclined to turn again to catch one more glimpse of the kindly face. A little farther on we see a young girl, with a look so joyous and happy, so entirely free from care, that we are impelled to search for the rosy glasses through which she views life. Time, the dispeller of all golden hued visions, has left her mind untouched, and she retains the joyous dreams of youth.

There is another with a look of discontent, amounting to almost misery. The rose-colored glasses have been broken early, and she is gazing through the murky, cloudy atmosphere of discontent. Another young girl is passing, and look closely! her face is a study, with its varying expression, reflecting every passing mood, then gay, now sad. The world either hardens or breaks the heart. Which process is her heart undergoing? In a few years, meeting her again, the face will be the page on which the story will be written in full, either in sombre tints or golden gleams.

Once more look at the daintily dressed woman coming down the street. She was made for sunshine and happiness, adversity would kill her. There are women who give one the impression that they should have all the good gifts which the gods provide, should be carefully looked after, tenderly cared for, they will share your joys, but no need to tell them your sorrows, for what can they know of sorrow? they whose feet have always travelled in smooth places. Refinement of manner and delicacy of feeling are essential qualities for every lady; but spare us the "dainty" woman. In hospitals there are women, educated and refined, who witness sights daily which cause them to sicken and shudder, but they are none the less refined, because they look upon the suffering of some poor mortal, none the less ladies, because they assist in alleviating the distress of their own kind. But "dainty," they can not be, thank heaven! It is the dainty woman who, if she sees a diseased, shabbily dressed mortal in trouble, passes quickly to the other side for fear of contamination, if she sees a child in distress hesitates, before offering help, to see if it is cleanly, and then the hand she offers is so nerveless, helpless and life-less, so weak and vacillating that perhaps it would have been just as well had she gone on her dainty way.

Again there are people who shut themselves in an armour of selfishness, im-pervious alike to gaunt poverty and hollow-eyed sorrow. From the crown of their heads to the soles of their feet is their world, they can neither see nor hear beyond it. The good qualities of their neighbors are seen through the large end of a tele-scope, appearing very small and a long way off, while their own are magnified until they at last look upon themselves as being the personification of all that is good and holy, and it is very amusing to study such a one, to watch her man-ner of addressing others. From the lofty pedestal of her own conceit, she allows some poor mortal to approach her shrine, but her manner says, "so far shalt thou come and no farther." Of what is she afraid? Has she fear of contamination? Is her goodness and purity of such a perishable nature that she fears pollution? Do not fear. If you possess innate goodness and womanly qualities you can pass through dangers unharmed, you can walk in the midst of sin and it will not touch you, you can take the hand of vice and it will leave no stain. From the height of your own purity do not look with scorn upon some less fortunate mortal, do not turn away in disgust, but examine closely, and underlying the outer crust of wickedness and sin, you will be astonished at the amount of good you can find, even in the most depraved. The human heart is a strange compound, made up of love and hate, of joy and sorrow, hope and despair, and who is able to read it? Who is able to un-derstand the sorrows, struggles and temptations of others, and who is competent to take upon himself the task of judging?

Every beat of the heart gives us a glimpse, either of heaven inspired love, or hell-born hate, of the sun-lit river of joy, or the gloom of sorrow, the golden gleam of hope or the stagnant pool of despair. Is it not strange that in all the workings of nature there is complete harmony; the whispering trees, the murmuring winds, the lowing herds, all speak a language of their own, while man is the only animal which makes war with his kind? The love of riches, the desire of gain, the pride of ambition takes possession of his mind to the exclusion of all else. In battle, soldiers walk over the dead bodies of friends and foes alike, unmoved, the only thought, the only desire is to win; the groans of the dying are drowned in the exultant shouts of the living as they find themselves victorious. In the battle of life there are many who, in their desire to win at all hazards, walk over the bodies of fallen ene-mies, and heed not the groans of even their friends. In all this worry and strife, all the weariness of body and brain, how few stop to enquire of themselves the means they are taking to attain their aim. Some have taken a step higher by walking over the body of a brother who has fallen by the wayside, wearied and heart sore, and if he succeeds in reaching the top-most rung of the ladder, envious tongues and slanderous epithets will reach him there, while if he falls he will carry with him the sneers and taunts of his fellow men. In this vast universe there is room for all, no need to jostle and crowd your neighbor. If he succeeds, while you fail, it will not better your condition to slander and vilify; if he fails while you win you will never regret having offered the hand in good will and fellowship. Many a heart has been softened, many a burden made lighter, by a few kind, cheerful words. There are none so low, none so degraded, as to be beneath consideration. To take the hand of the hardest criminal will not contaminate—vice is not contagious.

Joaquin Miller says:

> Is it worth while that we jostle a brother,
> Bearing his load on the rough road of life?
> Is it worth while that we jeer at each other,
> In blackness of heart that we war to the knife?
> God pity us all in our pitiful strife.
>
> God pity us all as we jostle each other,
> God pardon us all for the triumph we feel,
> When a fellow goes down 'neath his load on the heather
> Pierced to the heart by words keener than steel
> And mightier far for woe than for weal.
>
> Were it not well, in his brief little journey,
> On over the isthmus, down into the tide,
> We give him a fish instead of a serpent,
> Ere folding the hands to be and abide
> Forever, and aye, in dust at his side?
>
> Look at the roses saluting each other;
> Look at the herds all in peace on the plain,
> Man, and man only, makes war on his brother
> And laughs in his heart at his perils and pain,
> Shamed by the beasts that go down on the plain.
>
> It is worth while that we battle to humble
> Some poor fellow down into the dust?
> God pity us all! Time too soon will tumble
> All of us together, likes leaves in the gust,
> Humbled, indeed, down into the dust.

A woman was speaking who was dressed in soft white which clung to her slight form, and gave one the idea of a statue; a Galatea without a soul.

Fatalism had wound its slimy folds about her and she was unable to free herself from its chilling embrace. There is an old German legend which runs thus,

"Vineta was an old fortified place by the sea and the capital of an ancient nation. Her dominion extended over the neighboring coasts and over the waves where she ruled supreme. Unparallelled in splendor and greatness, countless treasures flowed in to her from other lands, but pride presumption and the sins of her inhabitants brought down the chastisement of Heaven upon her and she sank, swallowed up by the waves." The sailors still affirm that the fortress of Vineta lies uninjured at the bottom of the sea. They say that deep down in the water, they catch a glimpse of towers and cupolas, hear the bells ring, and at enchanted hours, the whole fairy city rises out of the depths and shows itself to a favored few. The old legend tells us that the one who has once looked on the lost Vineta, has once heard the sounds of her bells, is pursued all his life by a longing which bears him no rest until the enchanted city rises before him once more—or draws him down below unto the depths. The unfortunate person who has once gazed upon the ghastly ruins of Fatalism, knows no peace, but like the legend of Vineta, it will drag him down to misery and destruction.

The lady was saying:

We are but clay in the hands of the potter. Nothing we do can change the current of our lives. The hand of Fate is over all, leading us on, whether it be for good or for ill. From the cradle to the grave, from birth to death, there is a power ruling our destinies. In infancy our cradles are rocked by the invisible hand of fate, in middle age we are driven by it, in old age we are led by the same hand. I see before me a vessel starting out under full sail. The sky is clear; the air soft and balmy, and everything speaks of a favorable voyage, but when in mid-ocean, the sky grows dark, the wind arises, the waves roll higher and higher; soon the vessel gets beyond control, and the sailors find themselves drifting towards the breakers. Efforts are redoubled, all that human energy can do is done, but of no avail. Fate is beckoning them onward to their doom. We see a boy starting out in life full of youthful hopes and buoyant in health, happiness and strength. He sees in his mind's eye a thousand chances of success. Life is before him and there is one haven he must reach before his ambition is gratified. About midway in his career he stops. Clouds gather and he finds he has been driven from his course by adverse winds and tides—struggle as he may his efforts are futile for fate has intervened. The hand of destiny has led him, perhaps to misery, perchance to happiness, but which-ever it proves to be, he finds there is a hand, shaping, ruling, guiding, and that is the hand of Fate.

Lector House believes that a society develops through a two-fold approach of continuous learning and adaptation, which is derived from the study of classic literary works spread across the historic timeline of literature records. Therefore, we aim at reviving, repairing and redeveloping all those inaccessible or damaged but historically as well as culturally important literature across subjects so that the future generations may have an opportunity to study and learn from past works to embark upon a journey of creating a better future.

This book is a result of an effort made by Lector House towards making a contribution to the preservation and repair of original ancient works which might hold historical significance to the approach of continuous learning across subjects.

HAPPY READING & LEARNING!

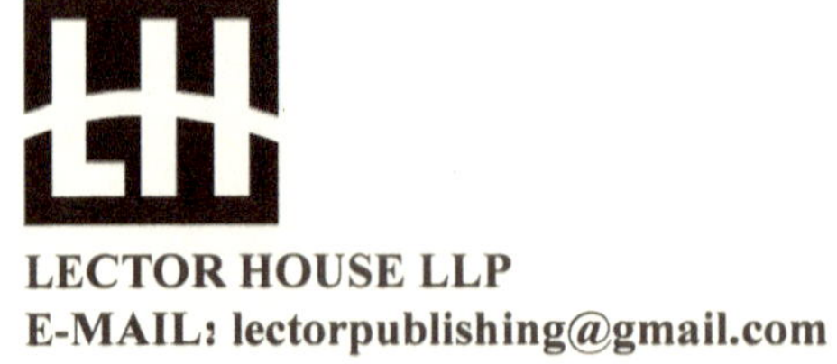

LECTOR HOUSE LLP
E-MAIL: lectorpublishing@gmail.com

www.ingramcontent.com/pod-product-compliance
Lightning Source LLC
LaVergne TN
LVHW090011200726
843493LV00004B/863

* 9 7 8 9 3 5 4 2 0 6 9 4 8 *